AM I STUCK IN THIS PRACTICE?

A Guide on Non-Compete Agreements for Doctors, Nurses, Dentists, and Other Health Care Providers

PETER J. GLENNON, ESQ.

The Glennon Law Firm, P.C.
GLENNONLAWFIRM.COM

The Glennon Law Firm P.C., USA, Publisher
www.glennonlawfirm.com

AM I STUCK IN THIS PRACTICE? A Guide on Non-Compete Agreements for Doctors, Nurses, Dentists, and Other Health Care Providers, First Edition. Copyright © 2022 by Peter J. Glennon, Esq.

All rights reserved. Printed in the United States of America. No part of this book may be used or reproduced in any manner whatsoever without the written permission of the author.

FIRST EDITION
ISBN 979-8-9852691-0-9

Without limiting the rights under copyright reserved above, no part of this publication may be reproduced, stored in or introduced into a retrieval system, or transmitted in any form or by any means (electronic, mechanical, photocopying, recording, or otherwise) without the prior written permission of both the copyright owner and the publisher of this book.

The scanning, uploading, and distribution of this book via the Internet or other means without permission from the owner and publisher is illegal and punishable by law. Please purchase only authorized electronic editions and do not participate in or encourage electronic piracy of copyrighted materials. Your support of the author's rights is appreciated.

For information please write the publisher:

The Glennon Law Firm, P.C.
160 Linden Oaks
Rochester, NY 14625

LEGAL DISCLAIMER

The general information in this book is not, nor is it intended to be, specific legal advice. Consult an attorney for specific legal advice regarding your individual situation and circumstances.

This book is provided as a general reference work and is for informational purposes only. You are advised to check for changes to current law and to consult with a qualified attorney on any legal issue. The receipt of or use of this book does not create an attorney-client relationship with The Glennon Law Firm, its principals, or any of its attorneys.

Because this book was prepared for general readership without investigation into the facts of each particular case, it is not legal advice. Neither The Glennon Law Firm nor any of its attorneys has an attorney-client relationship with you. The thoughts and commentary about the law contained in this book are provided merely as a public service and do not constitute solicitation or legal advice.

While we endeavored to provide accurate information in this book, we cannot guarantee that the material provided herein is accurate, adequate, or complete. This general legal information is provided on an 'as is' basis. We make no warranties and disclaim liability for damages resulting from its use. Legal advice must be tailored to the specific circumstances of each case and laws are constantly changing. Therefore, nothing provided in this book should be used as a substitute for the advice of competent legal counsel.

The material in this book may be considered advertising under applicable rules.

ACKNOWLEDGEMENTS

This Glennon Guide is dedicated to the best employment attorney I know, my wife Kimberly A. Glennon, Esq., and to our four children for inspiring and motivating me to write this book.

I also acknowledge and thank Laura Valade, Esq., whose creative input and editing helped translate my vision for this book into reality. And I thank Tim Cook for his friendship and creative assistance just when I needed it.

CONTENTS

ABOUT THE AUTHOR	14
HOW TO USE THIS BOOK	17
1. INTRODUCTION	19
Why Are You Reading This Book?	
2. GENERAL OPTIONS: NEGOTIATE, LITIGATE, STRATEGIZE	31
What Can I Do With My Non-Compete Agreement?	
3. ENFORCEMENT OF NON-COMPETE AGREEMENTS	47
Can My Employer Really Stop Me from Practicing My Profession Somewhere Else?	
4. COST OF NEGOTIATING, LITIGATING, OR STRATEGIZING	67
How Can I Beat the Non-Compete? (And How Much Would It Cost?)	
5. OTHER RESTRICTIVE COVENANTS	73
What Are the Other Restrictive Covenants and Why Are They Important?	
6. NEW PRACTICE, NEW CONSIDERATIONS	81
What Should I Do When Leaving One Practice for the Next?	
7. DISCRIMINATION IN A NUTSHELL	91
What About Discrimination in the Workplace?	
8. CONCLUSION: SUGGESTIONS TO AVOID NON-COMPETE ISSUES	97
When Should I Contact an Attorney?	

CONTENT DETAIL

1. INTRODUCTION: 19
Why Are You Reading This Book?

- First Scenario ... 19
- Second Scenario ... 20
- Third Scenario ... 21
- Why I Wrote This Book ... 21
- What Is a Non-Compete Agreement? ... 22
- What Are the Components of a Non-Compete Agreement? ... 23
- Is the Non-Compete Provision in the Contract Enforceable? ... 23
- How Is the Employer Protected From Loss? ... 24
- What Is the Geographical Proximity Challenge? ... 26
- How Do We Analyze the Three Starting Point Scenarios? ... 27

2. GENERAL OPTIONS: 31
NEGOTIATE, LITIGATE, STRATEGIZE
What Can I Do With My Non-Compete Agreement?

- When and What Should I Tell My New Employer? ... 31
- How the Court Analyzes a Non-Compete Agreement ... 32
- Negotiating the Non-Compete Agreement ... 34
- Develop a Negotiation Strategy ... 34
- Negotiating Employer's Release ... 35
- Notice Of Resignation ... 36
- Attorney Representation ... 36
- Litigating the Non-Compete Agreement ... 37
- Two Main Questions ... 37
- Legitimate Business Reason ... 38
- Overbroad and Blue Penciling ... 39

What Are Your Litigation Options? ... 39

Sue Your Employer ... 39

Employer Sues You ... 40

Case Pending in Court ... 41

Why Would Your Employer Fight Against You in Court? ... 42

Strategizing the Non-Compete Agreement ... 42

Conclusion ... 44

3. ENFORCEMENT OF NON-COMPETE AGREEMENTS 47
Can My Employer Really Stop Me from Practicing My Profession Somewhere Else?

Is the Non-Compete Enforceable? ... 47

1. Employer's Legitimate Business Interests ... 48

2. Non-Competes in New York ... 49

What If I'm Laid Off or Fired? ... 51

3. "For Cause" Termination ... 52

4. Laid-Off or Terminated Without Cause and Severance Payments ... 53

Employee Choice Doctrine Is a Legal Theory That May Affect You ... 54

What If My Contract Is Expiring? ... 55

How Is the Non-Compete Affected by the Agreement's Expiration? ... 55

What If My Compensation Was Reduced or My Compensation Model Was Changed? ... 56

1. Ratification and Rescission ... 56

2. Constructive Discharge ... 57

Why Are Some Non-Competes Enforceable and Others Not? ... 57

Why Did That Health Care Professional Beat Their Non-Compete, But I Can't? ... 58

(CHAPTER 3 Cont.)

    Unique Factual Analysis ... 58

    Language Of Agreement ... 59

    Practice Areas ... 60

    Other Issues or Considerations... 62

    I Know People. Should I Call Them? ... 62

    What Does It Mean to Come Up With a Plan? ... 63

    Be Careful with Friendships ... 63

4. COST OF NEGOTIATING, LITIGATING, OR STRATEGIZING   67
How Can I Beat the Non-Compete?
(And How Much Would It Cost?)

    Seeking Release From the Non-Compete Agreement ... 67

    1. Cost of Negotiating ... 68

    2. Cost of Litigating ... 69

    Pre-Trial Temporary Restraining Order (TRO) ... 69

    3. Cost of Strategizing ... 70

    How Much Am I Willing to Spend to Get Out of the Non-Compete? ... 71

    How Do the Numbers Add Up? ... 71

5. OTHER RESTRICTIVE COVENANTS   73
What Are the Other Restrictive Covenants and Why Are They Important?

    Non-Solicitation of Patients ... 73

    What Does It Mean to Not Solicit Patients? ... 73

    What Acts Are Permissible? ... 74

    What If My Patient Reaches Out to Me? ... 74

    What About Keeping Patients Informed? ... 75

    How Long Will This Go On? ... 76

    Non-Solicitation Of Employees ... 77

What Is Non-Solicitation Of Employees? ... 77

What If Former Co-Workers Respond to My New Employer's Job Vacancy Announcements? ... 77

Medical Practice Owners ... 78

What If I Own an Interest in the Practice and Want to Leave? ... 78

What If I Am a Practice Partner? ... 78

Non-Compete in the Employment Agreement ... 78

Non-Compete in the Buy-Sell Agreement ... 79

The Little Known Mohawk Doctrine ... 79

6. NEW PRACTICE, NEW CONSIDERATIONS 81
What Should I Do When Leaving One Practice for the Next?

1. Have a Plan ... 82

When and How Do I Give Notice to My Employer? ... 82

When and How Do I Inform Patients of My Move to the New Practice? ... 83

Limitations on Advertising and Marketing ... 85

Patient Records and Medical Progress Notes ... 85

Can I Bring My Patient Records With Me? ... 85

Records Transfer Procedure ... 85

2. Be Prepared to Answer the Employer's Questions and Make Your Presentation as Innocuous as Possible ... 86

3. Do Not Solicit Patients While Still Employed (or Face the Risk of Violating the Faithless Servant Doctrine) ... 87

What Is New York's Faithless Servant Doctrine? ... 87

4. Do Not Talk to Colleagues About Leaving ... 88

7. DISCRIMINATION IN A NUTSHELL 91
What About Discrimination in the Workplace?

Is All Discrimination or Retaliation at the Workplace Unlawful? ... 92

(CHAPTER 7 Cont.)

    What Are Protected Categories? ... 92

    Has the Employer's Behavior Risen to the Level of Actionable Discrimination? ... 93

    How Is Unlawful Retaliation Tied to Employment Discrimination? ... 94

    How Else Could Discrimination Law Apply to Non-Competes? ... 96

    Do I Need an Attorney? ... 96

8. CONCLUSION: SUGGESTIONS TO AVOID NON-COMPETE ISSUES   97
When Should I Contact an Attorney?

    First Scenario ... 97

    Second Scenario ... 97

    Third Scenario ... 98

    What If I'm Negotiating an Agreement Now? ... 98

    What If I Already Have an Agreement? ... 99

ABOUT THE AUTHOR

Peter J. Glennon, Esq.

Top Litigator.
Veteran.
Community Leader.

Peter J. Glennon, Esq., draws on his unique combination of business insight and legal experience to help today's professionals and business owners avoid problems, resolve disputes, and protect their assets. Peter has extensive litigation experience in state and federal courts, as well as in administrative venues, including such matters as: business divorces, contract disputes, professional and executive employment law, higher education employment law, trust and estate litigation, and high-asset divorce and equitable distribution matters.

Peter served as a law clerk for the Hon. Elizabeth W. Pine, Associate Justice of the New York Supreme Court, Appellate Division, Fourth Department, and as an extern law clerk to the Honorable David R. Homer, Federal Magistrate, Northern District of New York.

Peter J. Glennon, Esq.

Retiring with more than 24 years of military service, Peter is a former Deputy Staff Judge Advocate and served as a Squadron Commander, where he oversaw all the business operations of a military logistics center – a role that included managing a staff of more than 100 people. This unique business perspective helps him understand the demands facing today's professionals, executives, and business owners.

However, it is Peter's genuine commitment to service and creating strategies and successful outcomes for clients that makes him an ideal advocate both inside and outside the courtroom. Peter is co-founder and Board Chairman of Honor Flight Rochester, Inc., a non-profit organization that provides complimentary trips for World War II and other veterans to Washington, D.C., to tour their memorials. In addition, he was the 2020-2021 president of the Rochester Rotary Club, the 15th largest Rotary Club in the world, and he remains a member of its Trust Board.

Peter has been recognized repeatedly in Best Lawyers in America® and in Super Lawyers®, and was recently named one of the "Power 20 Employment Litigators." The litigation firm that he built, The Glennon Law Firm, P.C., is repeatedly listed as a U.S. News "Best Law Firm." He previously was recognized by the Rochester Business Journal as a "40 Under 40"; previously served on the Monroe County Bar Association Board of Trustees, and is a member of several bar associations.

Peter lives in Pittsford with his wife, Kimberly A. Glennon, Esq., their four children, and their dog Ford.

AM I STUCK IN THIS PRACTICE?

Am I Stuck In This Practice?

You don't have to be. This Glennon Guide provides the basic information you need to consider your options and to chart your course to your next destination. You remain the captain of your ship.

Am I Stuck In This Practice? was written to provide general information for health care professionals about health care employee rights in New York State under non-compete agreements and related topics. Maintaining control over your professional career is very important. Hopefully this Glennon Guide will assist you in doing so. Of course, this book does not contain legal advice and you should contact an employment attorney experienced in this area to obtain actual legal advice about your specific situation.

How to Use this Glennon Guide

You may of course read this book cover to cover, as the information is provided in a building block fashion. However, doing so is not necessary. The book is organized by topic and addresses the various questions that will arise as you grapple with your non-compete. Feel free to skip around and use the book as a reference, a starting point for you to understand what you may be facing, as a framework for which to analyze your situation, and to assess what steps you can take to *not get stuck in that practice*.

For additional helpful information and downloads about this topic, please visit www.AmIStuckInThisPractice.com.

For information about other topics in our Glennon Guide series, please visit www.GlennonGuides.com.

CHAPTER 1

INTRODUCTION

Why Are You Reading This Book?

As a busy health care professional with presumably significant time constraints, there must be a good reason why you chose to read *Am I Stuck In This Practice?*

Do you feel unappreciated at your current practice? Being unappreciated at work for your talents, skills, and dedication to patients can be distressing – especially when you are unappreciated by an employer who does not have a good relationship with you. Or when an employer impedes your ability to provide for your family and achieve personal and professional goals and dreams. In any event, educating yourself about non-compete agreements is always a good idea before entering into one and is always wise before changing positions.

As an employment law attorney, my experience tells me your situation probably fits into one of three scenarios.

First Scenario:

You are getting ready to sign your first (or a new) employment agreement containing a restrictive covenant or non-compete. Before committing to this agreement, you want to first know how the restrictions might apply to you and, second, how the restrictions will affect your professional career options further down the road.

As a resident or at white coat ceremonies you likely heard stories from family, friends, and peers about good and not so good experiences with non-compete agreements. Naturally, a lot of questions may run through your mind. "What will my position be like?" "Will I like this employer?" "If I don't like this employer – initially or years from now – what will the restrictions mean for me and my career?" Or you or your colleagues have experienced the headaches of leaving one practice to join another and do not wish to experience those headaches again.

Second Scenario:

Although currently employed, you want to better understand an agreement because you are contemplating leaving. Whether this is your first or 15th employment agreement, the terms "restrictive covenant" and "non-compete" are front and center. The ink was dry on the agreement years ago and, looking at the big picture, it's time for a job change. You want to be challenged, to do something different, to change the course you're on. Advancing your career at a new practice may require moving somewhere else.

Having developed a reputation and professional network, opportunities are coming your way with flattering overtures from other employers. You wonder, "What are my options?" "Can I leave?" "What potentially negative consequences could throw a blanket on my vision for the future?" You are focused on the legal issues and how they can be addressed and resolved. If this is your situation, then compliance and risk of breach are genuine concerns with tangible consequences.

Third Scenario:

You had some communications with your current employer about leaving for a new position, but were likely told you cannot work where you would like to go due to a non-compete agreement. Alternatively, you already resigned your position and now learn there will be more challenges in obtaining employment than you anticipated due to a non-compete agreement.

If you already quit your position or joined the competition, then you may be in hot water already. Are you staring down potential legal action for allegedly violating the terms of your prior employment contract? In that event, talk to an attorney soon about protecting your rights and interests.

Finding yourself in any of those three situations can be very stressful. We are talking about your profession, your livelihood, and your future, after all. Whichever scenario applies to you, this book will provide a general overview. We lay the groundwork of information in this book so you may have a framework to start educating yourself on your situation and analyzing your options.

The bottom line? Whatever your concerns are about the future, reading this book is a big step toward ensuring your career path continues on your terms.

Why I Wrote This Book

In writing *Am I Stuck In This Practice?* my purpose was to provide useful information that helps you frame the issues you are facing and be in a better position to pose questions to your attorney. I wanted to help you better understand the analysis an attorney would bring to your case. The information provided in these chapters will also make discussions with your spouse and other family members easier, understandable, and more productive. Lastly, I wanted to help you get out of one employment position and get into a new one.

Whatever your current situation and career plans, use *Am I Stuck In This Practice?* to advance toward your goals. Be mindful, the information provided in here is no substitute for specific legal advice from a competent attorney.

At The Glennon Law Firm, P.C., our employment law attorneys assist clients in negotiating, litigating, and strategizing around non-compete agreements and other restrictive covenants in professional and executive employment contracts. We do this for both the employees and the employers; so, we have the experienced wisdom from seeing both sides of the equation. Typically, a negotiated resolution is best and most cost-efficient. Litigation is sometimes necessary to protect our clients' interests, including temporary restraining orders (TROs), preliminary injunctions, and trials. But there are cases in which strategizing your career path around a non-compete is possible. All of these topics are touched on in later chapters, but let's go over a few key concepts first. (Please note that we use the terms "contract" and "agreement" interchangeably throughout this book.)

What Is a Non-Compete Agreement?

Basically, a non-compete agreement is a clause or provision in an employment contract between parties, the employee and the employer, that states that you will not work for a competitive practice for a certain amount of time in a specified geographic area.

What Are the Components of a Non-Compete Agreement?

Three components generally make up the non-compete agreement. By signing on the dotted line, the individual agrees that upon leaving said employment he or she will refrain from:

(a) Engaging in certain types of employment,

(b) In a certain geographic area,

(c) For the duration of a specified time period.

In other words, the parties agree that when or if employment is terminated, the health care professional will not work for the competition or benefit the competition until the stated time-period has expired. (In *Chapter 2* we discuss these components in greater depth.)

The purpose of these restrictions is to protect the employer's *legitimate business interests*. This is not to be taken lightly. Violating the agreement may be construed as a material breach of contract. This brings us to the question of whether the non-compete agreement can be enforced against the health care professional.

Is the Non-Compete Provision in the Contract Enforceable?

Yes, a non-compete provision is generally enforceable. However, enforceability is not a given, even with the most well-intentioned agreement. The terms of a non-compete clause must be worded very specifically. The employment contract should not be weak or vague. The geographical coverage cannot be overly broad. The specified time period must be of a reasonable duration. And there needs to be a *legitimate business interest* in order to enforce the agreement.

Generally, a court may find the restrictive covenant enforceable if the agreement:

- Does not pose a public harm,
- Is not overly burdensome on the employee,
- Is reasonable in terms of location and time, and
- Addresses the legitimate business concerns for the employer.

In a lawsuit, these questions are determined by the court. An incorrectly drafted or one-size-fits-all contract template not drafted by an attorney could result in the agreement being unenforceable. If the contract provision is unenforceable, then the health care professional may have the right to leave and work elsewhere without worrying about the restrictions.

How Is the Employer Protected From Loss?

Looking at this from the employer perspective, because of the time, effort, and resources invested to build and grow a practice or any company, many owners will take action against an employee, partner, or other individual who decides to leave the organization and take their experience, knowledge, and training (and patients or customers) obtained from the employer directly to a competitor. Generally, it is through non-compete agreements that companies and organizations seek to protect themselves from loss.

More specifically, the concern is with:

- Loss of customers, clients, or patients;
- Loss of employees;
- Loss of confidential information;
- Loss of competitive advantage; and
- Loss of trade secrets and other intellectual property.

While non-compete agreements can be valuable to protect the professional practice or business, they may also be unenforceable under New York law or public policy. Here, our focus is on the health care professions, including medical doctors, physician assistants, nurse practitioners, dentists, and others employed in the health care industry. Many of these principles are the same across industries, but not always. Accordingly, the analysis may vary with the business, profession, industry, or state involved. This book is for informational purposes only and does not substitute counsel or advice from an experienced attorney.

For the health care professional, a non-compete agreement may limit the list of practice options available to you. You may not have the legal right to use the special knowledge you've worked so hard to acquire when and where you desire.

This may seem unfair, overly burdensome, and career destroying. The fact is, the non-compete agreement can prohibit you from contacting or soliciting business from an employer's patients, customers, and other employees. It can prohibit you from providing services to them, as well. It can also prohibit you from soliciting other employees to join you, perhaps, even after they have left their positions with the same employer.

What Is the Geographical Proximity Challenge?

In a practical sense, when many health care providers are in relatively close proximity geographically, the act of changing jobs can be far more challenging. Where can you go?

In the Rochester, New York area, for example, health care is the number one industry and employer. There are other similar regions with large health care employers throughout New York State. Any non-compete negotiation has to apply the unique facts of that situation to the law. This is particularly important to those in the medical profession.

Consider this example. Anytown, USA, is divided into quadrants and each quadrant has its own professional areas. All the doctors practice in Q1. All the dentists in Q2. All the financial money managers, accountants, and stockbrokers in Q3. All the engineers and architects in Q4. In those circumstances, finding new employment in the same geographic area, in the same quadrant, may be quite difficult. Actually, it may be nearly impossible to find a new employer that does not compete with an existing or former employer.

Looking at the medical quadrant in Rochester, New York, there may be two large health care providers or health care systems and their hospitals. Consequently, there are numerous medical practices located in the same building, with even more across the street. They are concentrated in one area. When we discuss the requirements of non-competes – geographic scope and temporal scope – those realities matter significantly. And that saturation can be a geographical challenge.

How Do We Analyze the Three Starting Point Scenarios?

The analysis for health care professionals in each of the three scenarios discussed at the opening of this chapter is the same. Whether you are about to sign your first or a new employment agreement, are in the middle of a contract and considering changing jobs, or if you have already left your employer, what differs in the analysis is timing the *strategic approach* to resolving the issues. At our law firm, we discuss various strategies for the client to consider. By learning about the options, clients can take more control of their careers.

Are you just about to sign an agreement? Talk to an attorney about your plans to determine whether negotiation of the terms can or should still occur.

Are you in the middle of a contract and thinking through available options? Now is a great time to plan ahead. An ounce of prevention really is worth a pound of cure.

Are you ready to walk out the door? Did you already resign? Are you being told you cannot practice where you want to go? Now you have less room to maneuver, but you still have options. It's time to consult an attorney.

As you read each chapter, remember that the employment agreement is a contract just like any other. Yes, some special rules apply to non-competes for health care professionals, but we still utilize a basic contract analysis. Understand that in analyzing any contract there are legalities and there are realities. On one hand, we have the legalities: these are laws, theories, and never-ending hypotheticals ("What if I move my practice 50 miles away?"). On the other hand, we have the realities: assessing a cost-benefit analysis for the time, money, and frustration involved, and your career path.

What we do at The Glennon Law Firm is analyze both sides of the ledger, the legalities and realities. In our experience, where those paths intersect in the individual's case is usually where we find the better solution and the best way out. The law may dictate the terms of what can and cannot be done, but we also need to be realistic because we are dealing with people. This is about you, your career, your profession, your family, and your life.

We also must be considerate of the employer. There are sound reasons for why non-compete agreements exist. That is not to say, however, that every articulated purpose is justified. Some restrictions have no reason for inclusion, yet there they are.

At our law firm, we assess the legalities and realities of your unique situation. We assess your goals and challenge you to determine what your long-term goals truly are (without the distractions, anxieties, and emotional fall-out from your work situation). Then we build a strategy and chart a course forward for you to keep control.

As I've said to many clients facing these challenges, "When we see the path, you need only take my hand, put your head down, and follow me. We will get you through the forest. Yes, it can be a bumpy ride. But by planning appropriately, we can anticipate those bumps and get you over them, one by one."

We welcome your input. Please feel free to reach out to us at *(585) 210-2150* or at *info@GlennonLawFirm.com* with any questions.

CHAPTER 2

GENERAL OPTIONS: NEGOTIATE, LITIGATE, STRATEGIZE

What Can I Do With My Non-Compete Agreement?

Whether you have been bound by your employment contract for less than a year or for closer to a decade, you need to know about the generally available options you have to address any non-compete agreement issues.

When and What Should I Tell My New Employer?

Initially, it is important that you inform your new prospective employer about your non-compete agreement with your prior employer. Addressing these issues at the beginning of the relationship is always better, particularly while they are still very interested in hiring you. Having a non-compete does not disqualify you from accepting a new position. Instead, it allows for the new employer to review your agreement and determine for itself the possibility of any risk. Having them on your side from the start can be very helpful.

Initially, if your former employer seeks to stop you from working for a new employer, it will inevitably send a "cease and desist" letter to you. Your former employer will typically copy your new employer on the letter and may send a separate letter to your new employer, copying you, informing the new employer of your non-compete. Why? Because the former employer may have legal claims against the new employer for hiring you. In that event, it is common for the new employer to seek to avoid litigation by terminating your employment in order to cut its damages and build good faith with the former employer. If you do not disclose your non-compete in the first instance, you will most likely be terminated. That is why raising the issue and sharing your agreement with the new employer before changing positions is a good practice.

Sharing your agreement will avoid future litigation issues and may build an ally in your new employer (this could help you should the former employer actually pursue you later). Your new employer's legal counsel may even work with your employment attorney to assess the situation and devise the best strategy for you to move forward.

How the Court Analyzes a Non-Compete Agreement

To do something about your non-compete agreement so you may further your career elsewhere, you have three general options – negotiate, litigate, or strategize around it. In a moment, we'll take a closer look at each of these options and provide some examples. But first, we need to discuss how the court analyzes the non-compete agreement.

Without getting into the procedural aspects of a lawsuit (save that conversation for your attorney), there is something you need to understand now. (Here comes some "legalese.") The question before the court is typically a question of law, not a question of fact (unless there are disputed facts involved in analyzing the non-compete clause).

As a question of law, the court generally analyzes the contract and decides whether the employer has a legitimate business interest to protect and, if so, then whether the scope of the non-compete agreement is reasonable:

(1) In scope or breadth, and

(2) Scope of time (temporal duration), and

(3) In geography.

The initial question of whether a legitimate business interest exists in the health care industry is a fact-specific question for your attorney to consider. Many times, and for purposes of our discussion here, the *legitimate business interest* is present due to the "unique skills" of the healthcare professional. That is not always the case, though, so always consider this threshold issue.

As for the scope or breadth of the limitation, some medical non-competes state the doctor "cannot practice medicine" at all. Now, absent special circumstances, that is likely too broad a limitation and unenforceable. However, prohibiting a specialty (for example, dermatology) while allowing general practice would probably be sufficiently narrow in scope to pass judicial muster and be enforceable.

As for the "temporal scope" (the duration of time you are prohibited from competing), the time period is often "two years" and may be less. As for geographic scope, this is supposed to be the market area in which you practiced, so the distance may be "5 miles from any clinical practice location" or could be "50 miles." (Fifty miles is very rare, but at least one court in New York State upheld that distance based on the unique circumstances of that case.)

Now, let's discuss the three general options you have – negotiate, litigate, strategize – when furthering your career means you need to do something about your non-compete agreement.

Negotiating the Non-Compete Agreement

Negotiating involves exchanging value with your employer to be free from your non-compete agreement.

This could mean buying your way out of the contract. But the point is simply that you attempt to reach an agreement with your employer for your release. This release would allow you to work wherever you want in exchange for something of value to the employer or a sum of money paid to the employer, by either you or your new employer. The goal should be a deal that is satisfactory to you, your current employer, and your new employer. Effective negotiation requires a cost and risk analysis and will depend upon the parties' relationships. This will ultimately be a business decision for all involved.

Develop a Negotiation Strategy

You first need a negotiation strategy. An experienced attorney could help you devise your strategy. In any event, while of course you need to clearly define your own goals and red-line positions, you must also consider "What is the employer's business case for keeping or releasing you?" In other words, what's in it for them?

Does your employer need your particular services? Is it concerned with how long it might take to replace you? Does it need to set a precedent and make an example of you in order to discourage other employees from leaving? What costs and risks could your employer face if you were to challenge the agreement? These and many other questions should be considered by you in devising a strategy.

Employers are often willing to negotiate with health care professionals in order to avoid the cost of litigating in court. They are not fond of incurring legal fees and expenses, which will be a consideration for them. They also could be concerned about the risks associated with litigation. If you win, then other professionals with the same agreement could be free to leave without complying with the non-compete as well. They may not want to risk setting that precedent.

Negotiating Employer's Release

If the employer is comfortable letting you go because it believes your new position will *not* be substantially detrimental to their business, then the employer may agree to release you from the non-compete in exchange for something in return. This could be a confidentiality agreement, a non-solicitation of patients and employee agreement or, most likely, a sum of money from you, the health care professional.

The question of "How much should I pay?" will depend upon the unique facts of your situation. Both parties should weigh their respective pros and cons. What profit or benefit is there in settling? Would you pay the employer as much, less than, or more than what you would pay an attorney to litigate? Will you be earning greater compensation with your new employer, which could make a buyout of your non-compete a simple business expense?

In attempting to present its business case in the negotiation, the employer will bemoan Locums fees (temporary physician staffing), costs associated with replacing you (hiring and screening costs), and so on.

However, deterrence may be more important to the employer's business decision. Charging doctors for their release from a non-compete agreement is considered by some to be crucial in maintaining deterrence to other health care professionals from leaving. By charging you to free yourself from the non-compete, your employer is communicating to other practitioners, "Yes, it's possible to leave. But it will cost you."

Notice Of Resignation

Lastly, the notice of resignation provision in health care professional contracts typically requires between "90 days" to "six months" notice. No matter what you plan to do, you always have to meet the resignation notice provision or face other monetary consequences under your contract for leaving your employer early. But the timing of your departure may be another negotiation point that allows you to leave your non-compete obligations behind.

Attorney Representation

Should you hire an attorney to represent you in the negotiations? Maybe. It depends upon your unique circumstances. Discuss the situation with your attorney before taking action. Then make a practical, cost-benefit decision.

Of course, by effectively negotiating an employment agreement before signing it, with the goal of minimizing the scope of the non-compete clause, your current situation would be more favorable today. Hindsight is 20/20. But remember to seek competent legal advice before attempting to negotiate terms of an employment contract on your own. And certainly before announcing your departure!

Litigating the Non-Compete Agreement

Litigating involves going to court to prove your position and getting out of the non-compete agreement.

Litigation means resolving disagreement over the contract in court (or through arbitration). Is the non-compete clause invalid under the law? Such points will help you advance any negotiation strategy that you have (see above). And if you have the law and facts on your side, then you may go to court to litigate the issue with the goal of having the non-compete or other restrictive covenants thrown out or limited. If they are not eliminated entirely, then the court could narrow the scope of the non-compete clause's terms because it was written too broadly; effectively reducing the restrictions to you.

Working as a doctor, dentist, or other health care professional with a non-compete agreement does not mean the restrictive covenant will automatically be enforced by a court against you. There's more to the consideration.

Two Main Questions

Generally speaking, the two main questions that will be posed to determine whether the non-compete will be enforced will be:

> 1. Whether your employer has a legitimate business interest to protect by enforcing the agreement, and
>
> 2. Whether the non-compete agreement's terms are reasonable or not overly broad.

If there is no legitimate business interest, then the non-compete fails. If there is a legitimate business interest, but the non-compete terms are unreasonable, then the court will either throw the non-compete agreement out (as invalid and unenforceable) or limit or narrow its scope.

Legitimate Business Reason

What does "valid" mean? A valid non-compete agreement presumes the current employer has a "legitimate business reason" to enforce the terms against you. Examples of legitimate business reasons might include: The employer invested money in you, marketed and promoted you, and/or obtained patients for you to treat. Those investments could create a *legitimate business interest* that the court might allow the employer to protect. The employer's reason for the non-compete is not without limitation, though.

Whether choosing to litigate makes good business sense or is a matter of principle (or both), the lawsuit is sure to clarify your position. Your current employer will come to understand from the lawsuit that:

(1) You are leaving,

(2) You are taking a new job,

(3) You are more than happy to resolve the entire situation in a court of law by a judge (or by arbitration, if the agreement so dictates), and

(4) You are willing to spend the money on an attorney.

But remember, standing on principle, like litigation, is expensive.

Overbroad and Blue Penciling

When the non-compete terms are considered overbroad, the judge may fix the defect by narrowing the scope of the clause. This judicial re-write is an example of *"blue penciling"* a contract provision back to being valid and enforceable. (Refer to *Chapter 1's* discussion on contract validity.)

What Are Your Litigation Options?

Sue Your Employer

One option is to sue your employer in court for a declaratory judgment. This asks the judge to rule (declare) that the non-compete agreement is invalid and does not prevent you from freely changing employers.

Think of it this way, "Judge, please look at this contract. Make a final ruling so I don't have to keep speaking with my current employer. Rule that it is unenforceable or, if enforceable on its face, rule that it is unenforceable as it applies to me. Or at least narrow the terms to make it reasonable under the circumstances." This is the option you take when you and your attorney feel very confident in your possibility of success and going to court is viewed as the more time-efficient and cost-efficient means to resolving the situation.

When you commence this legal action, however, the employer would likely also sue you in response and ask the court for an injunction to stop you from going to the new employer. To support its request for this *temporary restraining order (TRO)* or preliminary injunction, the employer would have to present your agreement and demonstrate how you are violating it, whether drawing patients away or enticing employees to leave (if you also have a non-solicitation clause, which is typical), or that you are otherwise violating the non-compete agreement. It would likely argue that it is or will suffer economic harm as a consequence of your violating the non-compete agreement.

Employer Sues You

A second option is to not file for declaratory relief, but to wait and see if the employer is willing to go to court to stop you. This is more common and occurs when the employer believes strongly in its own position. In this option, the employer typically seeks a TRO and a preliminary injunction against you from the court.

The employer asks the court to examine the language of the agreement. Effectively, the employer would be saying: "Judge, you have to stop this doctor from going to a new employer. We have a valid, enforceable non-compete agreement and we need you to protect our *legitimate business interest*."

Under appropriate circumstances, the judge could prohibit you from going to the new employer. But many times, if the only possible damage to the employer is *lost revenue and profit*, then you, or you and your new employer, could be liable to pay those damages, but you would be permitted to start working at the new employer's practice.

The employer can also seek a declaratory judgment, asking the judge to rule, "the doctor is bound by this agreement" and must comply with its terms and pay any damages to the current employer.

Yes, your new employer could be sued in court in this situation, too. Which is why you should ensure that it is aware of your non-compete agreement prior to changing positions and consider your new employer's views of the situation prior to acting. Your attorney and the new employer's attorney should be communicating during these early stages of negotiation or litigation.

Case Pending in Court

With the case now pending in court, you likely will start working at the new position while the old employer challenges it in court. The case continues like a regular lawsuit, but you move on with your new job – unless the court issues an injunction against you stating that you cannot work for the new employer.

At trial, there are opportunities to argue how the terms as set forth in the document, when applied to your situation, are overly oppressive or *unfair to you*. If the court determines there was overreaching by the employer or the non-compete is overly broad, then it can throw-out the entire non-compete. And you never have to worry about it again.

Alternatively, the court may "blue pencil" the contract terms to make it comply with the law. Say, for example, the agreement's geographic restriction was "30 miles" and the temporal duration is "three years." The judge may blue pencil the agreement, changing it to "10 miles" and "two years." The agreement is valid and enforceable with the judge's changes. Of course, a party who disagrees with the judge's final decision may file a timely appeal. That is another business decision.

Why Would Your Employer Fight Against You in Court?

The employer is trying to protect its business. If the employer wins in court, then you will be ordered to pay damages to the employer. The damages would be based on profits that you gained and that the employer lost as a consequence of your change in employment. Lost profits could include expenses your employer had to pay for hiring temporary help, among other things. Lawsuits of this nature can be expensive with substantial legal fees for both sides, particularly if everyone moves quickly to race into court.

Strategizing the Non-Compete Agreement

Strategizing involves working around the non-compete agreement's terms to avoid its penalties.

Strategizing around the non-compete agreement may actually be the first thing you and your attorney do. If you are able to work around the limitations of the non-compete, then you will save time, money, and frustration as compared to negotiating or litigating with your employer. But know that even if you strategize around the non-compete terms, that you may end up having to negotiate or defend against the employer's litigation against you.

To strategize, first, review the terms of the agreement. What is the scope? How many years? How far away? Is it possible for you to comply with the terms of the agreement and free yourself? Complying with the agreement's terms would avoid giving your employer money to buy your way out and avoid the expense of trying to litigate your way out.

Assess your situation and the possibilities. Is the community where you live near another city or town? If the geographic limitation in the non-compete is "30 miles," for example, then ask yourself whether you could accept a position in a community 40 miles away? So long as you work around the non-compete for the requisite time period, all will be fine. The clock will run out and you'll never risk violating the non-compete.

In addition to treating patients, some non-compete agreements restrict the health care professionals' ability to teach medicine at a college or university. Such a covenant could be enforceable, depending upon the specific facts of the case. Strategize a work around.

Could you commute to a city just beyond the current employer's geographic area for the requisite duration? Maybe. Would it be inconvenient? Probably. Still, you would be advancing your career with the new employer. Because many employers are understanding of non-competes, you have an opportunity to create an advantageous work schedule with more time off.

Depending upon credentials and interests, you might remain local but not practice in your specific specialty. For instance, instead of practicing locally as a dermatologist for the requisite two years, you practice as a general practitioner. Or maybe work as a Locum or hospitalist for the duration of the non-compete. This isn't a novel approach; many health care professionals have acted this way successfully. For those who are able and willing, there are ways to work around an enforceable non-compete agreement.

Conclusion

There are two career moments at which you can best control the possible negative effects of a non-compete agreement:

1. *Before signing the agreement, and*
2. *Before announcing your departure.*

Before signing the agreement, you have an opportunity to negotiate more favorable terms in the non-compete clause. For example, perhaps explain your intent to relocate in two years to a neighboring town 40 miles away. In that situation, you might try negotiating the employer's geographic limit from "50 miles" down to "40 miles."

Learn what triggers the non-compete clause: Who? What? Where? When? How? Importantly, if you are laid off or terminated from your employment, then the non-compete clause will not likely be enforceable against you. But if you are terminated for cause, then it likely will be enforceable against you. Please re-read the preceding sentence!

After you have been working under the employment agreement, you need someone to analyze these issues and devise a plan before you actually resign from your position. Do not put yourself in a weak position by not thinking through these issues. Consult an attorney to help you map your exit from the practice before you act. You need someone capable of advising you and of helping you articulate your plans; someone to tell you what to say, when to say it, and when not to speak. And if need be, to take you by the hand and lead you out of the forest safely.

No, it's never too soon to think about how a non-compete agreement could affect your future. My best suggestion is to always plan a job change early. Ideally, before you even sign a non-compete agreement. Regardless, always consider your options. My second best suggestion is to always make a plan before giving notice to your employer!

With proper prevention, health care professionals can avoid being beholden to an employer, avoid litigating non-competes, and maybe even avoid having to buy out of the contract.

CHAPTER 3

ENFORCEMENT OF NON-COMPETE AGREEMENTS

Can My Employer Really Stop Me from Practicing My Profession Somewhere Else?

Maybe. The answer is not a clear-cut "Yes or No." While employers say every non-compete agreement is enforceable, employees think non-competes are never enforceable. The answer truly lies in the middle. It is a fact specific analysis.

There are rules governing the enforceability of non-compete agreements and some of those rules are particular to the medical profession. For this reason, enforceability depends upon the unique facts and circumstances of each individual case.

As attorneys, we frequently hear stories from health care professionals about a "friend of mine did this" or the "doctor I know did that." But no two cases are the same. Every professional, every situation, and every contract is unique. Even where the contract language is identical, the individuals could be practicing in different towns or jurisdictions, or under different management. All that being said, we need to determine whether the specific non-compete agreement at issue is enforceable.

Is the Non-Compete Enforceable?

Let's start with the meaning of the non-compete and how it can work. Typically, a non-compete means the health care professional (the employee) will not work for a business or start a new business that competes for the same patients or clients as the current employer does. In the law, this is known as a type of *restrictive covenant*. The restrictive covenant is part of the employment contract. Restrictive covenant is effectively the "umbrella" phrase for a list of actions from which an employee must refrain because of their employment agreement.

There are many types of restrictive covenants, including non-compete agreements, non-solicitation of patients, and non-solicitation of employees. Our focus here is on non-competes which the health care professional agrees not to work where those services are in competition with the current employer.

1. Employer's Legitimate Business Interests

The intention of the non-compete agreement is to protect the employer's "legitimate business interest." Yes, that is a legal phrase, but it boils down to identifying what the employer's legitimate interests are under the law. Are they identified? What might those interests be?

Generally, the employer's legitimate business interests may be viewed as money or assets invested in the health care professional, such as investment in marketing the particular doctor or dentist, or invested in training the employee if there are special training or certification classes. There are "legitimate business interests" in the employee's relationships developed by and through the employer's efforts, which may be through a medical practice, hospital, or university.

2. Non-Competes in New York

Non-competes in New York are not favored under public policy. However, in New York they are enforced to the extent necessary to protect the employer's legitimate business interest, but only when the non-compete is *reasonable in scope*.

Recall from *Chapter 2* that, to be reasonable in scope, the non-compete must:

> *1. Be reasonable in duration (amount of time for which the employee is agreeing not to compete as an employee or business owner of another entity), and*
>
> *2. Be reasonable in geographic scope (distance from primary practice area in which the professional is agreeing not to compete).*

If a legitimate business interest exists, then both of the above are required for a court to find a non-compete agreement to be valid and enforceable.

Also recall from *Chapter 2*, even the non-compete that is neither valid nor enforceable because it is found to be overly broad may be modified by a court, or "blue penciled," in order to make its terms enforceable under the law.

Within the medical profession particularly, courts in New York State have always considered physicians to have "unique skills" and to provide "extraordinary services." Therefore, in New York non-compete agreements may be enforced against doctors and blue-penciling may be more common than in other industries.

Enforceability of non-compete agreements by New York courts is interesting because some states, such as Massachusetts and California, have all but eradicated non-compete agreements. There is also talk of some action at the federal level to legislate away non-competes. In 2021, the District of Columbia passed a law prohibiting most non-compete agreements for medical professionals – with an exception for doctors earning $250,000 or more. Clearly, there is a business interest they are considering.

Time and again, courts in New York State hold non-compete agreements enforceable against doctors because they are considered to have unique skills and provide extraordinary services. In balancing the scales, the side of health care employers tends to receive greater weight as against doctors and medical professionals.

Consider how those scales balanced in the 1996 New York case of *Bollengier v. Gulati*, 233 A.D.2d 721 (3rd Dept 1996). In *Bollengier*, a young cardiovascular and thoracic surgeon had a contract in which the non-compete was limited to a geographical scope of the borders of the county in upstate New York where they were practicing. The time, or duration, of the non-compete was limited to two years.

The young surgeon, who was violating the non-compete agreement, had been with the employer for only one year, and had moved into that county solely to accept the position with the employer. When the parties were no longer getting along, the young surgeon quit and then attempted to compete directly with the former employer.

When the senior doctor sued the young surgeon to stop him from competing, the young surgeon argued how the public-at-large would be harmed if he was not allowed to offer his surgical skills in that county. However, the court found that the original surgeon was established in the area (for more than 30 years), that patients otherwise had access to necessary medical skills and treatments and, therefore, no harm to the public would result by enforcing the non-compete agreement against the young surgeon.

Yes, the *Bollengier* court found the non-compete enforceable because that employer's legitimate business interest included spending nearly 30 years building its practice and developing goodwill. (Yes, goodwill is a legitimate business interest.) The court further found the time and geographic limits in the non-compete agreement to be reasonable.

More often than not, a court will enforce a proper non-compete agreement against the health care professional. Does this mean that doctors are stuck or otherwise held back by these agreements? Not necessarily. Health care professionals do have options, as discussed later.

What If I'm Laid Off or Fired?

In the event the health care professional is laid off or fired – or leaves by any termination caused by the employer's preference or decision – then, most likely, the non-compete will *not* be enforceable against the employee in New York.

Restrictive covenants are not favored in New York because the courts do not want to impede a person's ability to work and provide for his or her family. Given this public policy preference, the courts look closely at non-competes and will typically scrutinize them against the employer.

In a situation where employment is terminated without cause by the employer, the employer is considered to have had the opportunity to protect any legitimate business interests it may have by not terminating the employee. Essentially, if the employer chooses to let the person go, then that was its business decision to make. Although the court is not likely to enforce any non-compete against the employee in that situation, it may enforce another restrictive covenant, such as a non-solicitation clause of patients or of other employees.

The court will enforce the confidentiality requirements of the employment agreement. Even in the absence of an employment agreement, current and past employees remain bound by confidentiality requirements under what is called "common law." You are not allowed to share with others, including new employers, confidential business plans (for example, marketing ideas) and other information that an employer tries to keep confidential as a competitive edge.

3. "For Cause" Termination

There is one caveat to not enforcing a non-compete agreement against an employee when the employer ends the relationship – that is *"for cause"* termination. If an employee is terminated for cause, then it is possible a New York court *will* enforce the non-compete against the employee.

For cause termination is usually defined in the employment agreement itself. Generally, it means the employee did something wrong, violated a work policy, or was convicted of a felony, among other things.

4. Laid-Off or Terminated Without Cause and Severance Payments

If the health care professional is terminated without cause or laid off, then the non-compete agreement will not likely be enforceable against him or her in New York. That is, unless the individual accepted a severance payment from the employer and signed an additional agreement.

The employee may exercise the choice to accept a severance payment (or some other consideration) from the employer in a new contract. The new contract typically includes a new non-compete provision, which could be enforceable.

Severance agreements or separation packages are commonly used in many industries and professions, particularly in the employment of health care professionals. Here is a basic analysis.

If the employee is being laid off, then typically the non-compete language in the employment agreement would not be enforced against him or her because the lay-off is not the employee's choice or fault. However, the employer may offer post-termination severance funds to the individual (perhaps a few weeks or months of compensation) in exchange for the severance or separation agreement being signed which, among other things, typically includes terms that provide for mutual releases for many legal claims or lawsuits – and can provide for restrictive covenants, including non-compete agreements.

Employee Choice Doctrine Is a Legal Theory That May Affect You

The "Employee Choice Doctrine" is effectively when the employee promises not to sue the employer for any claim and promises to abide by either the prior non-compete or a new non-compete, or other restrictive covenant. By signing such a document – the severance agreement or separation agreement – and accepting the compensation offered by the employer, the choice to be bound by the non-compete is then legally enforceable, even if the employer was laying off the employee. Other benefits could also be offered to the employee. In any event, this type of situation is generally referred to as the *"employee choice doctrine"* in the law. The employee has the choice to accept the benefits with the accompanying burdens, or not.

Notably, employers do not have to tell their employees (and usually don't) that by forgoing the severance or separation agreement and consideration, any prior non-compete agreement is invalid if the health care professional is being terminated without cause.

Consider, too, how termination tends to take people by surprise, even shock them. An employee may be pulled aside and told by the director of the medical department or by human resources that their work with the employer is over – it happens. The surprise factor then has the employee naturally thinking about how they'll get by financially in the short-term. Where will they get their next job? When? How will they pay their bills? So when a severance is dangled in front of them, it looks like easy money. In my practice, I've seen as little as $10,000 to $25,000 offered in severance. Frankly, the money just isn't worth it for the non-compete agreement in many situations.

What If My Contract Is Expiring?

Many times, health care agreements have an auto-renewal provision. Auto-renewal means the same terms of the written contract (including the non-compete terms) continue automatically unless either the employer or the employee provides written notice within a specified time period indicating that party does not choose to renew the agreement.

However, when the parties agree that the employment agreement is ultimately expiring, there is another clause to consider that explains which of the obligations continue post-termination (yes, it nearly always includes the non-compete obligation). That means that when your agreement expires by its own terms, you are typically bound by the non-compete provisions. You need to pay special attention to all of those provisions to ensure that you do not violate your promises or obligations under the agreement.

How Is the Non-Compete Affected by the Agreement's Expiration?

Your employment agreement likely has language to the effect of "while employed here and for 24 months after termination of employment" you will be bound by the non-compete. Yes, I have seen agreements where the non-compete is effective only while the professional is employed by the employer, but that is a very, very rare scenario.

What the post-termination obligation clauses mean is that when your employment agreement terminates or expires, then you are bound by the restrictive covenants, including the non-compete clause, for the stated period of time. This assumes that the agreement and non-compete clause are valid. But the point is that in the automatic termination, you were not terminated by the employer and you did not resign; rather, the employment agreement ended by operation of its own terms, which include your agreement to abide by the non-compete.

What If My Compensation Was Reduced or My Compensation Model Was Changed?

Reducing compensation does not usually invalidate a non-compete, particularly if the health care professional resigns. There is more to consider, however.

1. Ratification and Rescission

What if compensation was reduced, but the employee continued working under the new model? Arguably, the new model may have been *ratified*, including the compensation change, by the employee continuing to work for the employer.

Courts have held, however, that if the employee signed a non-compete agreement in exchange for a promotion and a pay raise, but the pay raise was cut after receiving the promotion, then the consideration for the non-compete may have been *rescinded*. Rescission effectively undoes the contract, invalidating the non-compete agreement. Before making any career decisions in such a situation, consult an attorney. This can be a very challenging factual analysis!

There is yet another possibility.

2. Constructive Discharge

A dramatic pay reduction could be considered a *constructive discharge*, which may be termination without cause. Thus, a dramatic pay reduction could have the same result as the employer laying off the professional. In that case, the non-compete would not be enforceable. But raise your displeasure about a pay reduction soon after it occurs.

If you wait too long to complain about the reduction, then you may ratify the reduction and lose the constructive discharge argument.

Why Are Some Non-Competes Enforceable and Others Not?

Even if we were all health care professionals working in the same university or large practice setting, each of us would still have unique circumstances. Enforceability depends upon specifics. What is the language of the non-compete? What are the person's circumstances? What is happening to that individual when looking to leave (work environment and conditions faced)? It is a fact-specific analysis. Your situation may be different from your colleagues.

Why Did That Health Care Professional Beat Their Non-Compete, But I Can't?

How can one health care professional beat the non-compete agreement, but another is forced to comply with the non-compete? Well, there are four bases for why outcomes differ from one case to the next:

- ◆ Unique factual analysis,
- ◆ Language of the agreement,
- ◆ Health care practice areas, and
- ◆ Other issues or considerations.

Let's take a closer look at each of these situations.

Unique Factual Analysis

There is always a unique factual analysis. This is about you, not some other person. Who are you? Where are you working? Where do you want to work? Where don't they want you to work?

What is the relevant market? In what community do you practice? If practicing in a rural area or remote hinterland, then older New York cases have allowed up to 50 miles as a permissible geographical limit for non-compete agreements. Why? Because there may not be many doctors in those geographical areas, which is the relevant market.

In considering a unique factual analysis, we look at the size of the relevant market and then seek to balance public policy concerns. We want to ensure people can work, which favors the employee. With health care, public policy is concerned with ensuring people can choose their providers and get the health care they need. We also balance the employer's legitimate business interest with these public policy concerns.

Language Of Agreement

As touched on earlier, to be enforceable an employer must have a legitimate business interest and the scope of the non-compete agreement must be reasonable in time and geography. Even in situations where one would assume all such agreements are uniform, they will likely vary. Not every agreement will be the same.

Despite working for the same employer, for instance, the language in your agreement may differ from another employee's agreement. An employer may have a new employment contract or new non-compete agreement, yet not require everyone to sign it; resulting in different language for different employees.

On a practical level, this means the more senior doctor might not have a non-compete, whereas the newly hired doctor could. Or the more senior-tenured health care professional may have a less restrictive non-compete (with a greater emphasis on non-solicitation, for instance), whereas the newer employee may have a more restrictive non-compete agreement. The language used in your specific agreement is what matters most!

When we say a non-compete agreement must be reasonable in scope and have a legitimate business interest, we are talking about *circumstances unique to each health care professional at the time the agreement is being analyzed in the community in which the professional practices.*

So, how do we determine reasonableness? Consider the rural physician practicing in an area where there are few doctors. In that instance, a more reasonable geographic scope may be 50 miles as was true several decades ago in a particular 1977 upstate New York case. But would 50 miles be considered reasonable today? That is doubtful.

Because of the employee's unique circumstances and requirement of reasonableness, there is no standard rule stating the time must be "two years or less" or the geography must be "10 miles or less." Determining reasonableness is a case-by-case analysis.

In addition to geographic distance, another challenge can arise in a densely populated community with, for example, a large university medical center where health care professionals are abundant. There may be one medical plaza, one development, one crossroad where all of the health care practices are situated. Which means the geographic area in the non-compete, even if limited to "three miles," may be seriously limiting. In a densely populated community, all the relevant practice areas could be located within those three miles. Those specific details must be considered in the enforceability of a health care professional's non-compete agreement.

Practice Areas

The health care provider's specific practice area or specialty may also impact a court's decision on whether the non-compete agreement is enforceable. Recently, this has become a more vigorously litigated issue.

Arguably, stating "the doctor cannot practice medicine" is overly broad. We have many specialties today, more than in previous decades. If you have a couple board certifications for different practice areas, then it may be possible to limit you in one practice area, allowing you to go to another practice area.

What about the physician who services numerous other health care professionals? The anesthesiologist, for example, effectively services many other doctors, possibly in different hospitals. They do not typically possess a physician-patient relationship, in the business sense.

If the anesthesiologist wishes to change practices, then what is the employer's legitimate business interest to stop them? Few, if any, patients name their anesthesiologist for an upcoming medical procedure. The anesthesiologist is not marketed by the employer and does not have a book of business that will follow the move. An employer's legitimate business interest is typically additional training or investments made in a particular health care professional.

Comparing the anesthesiologist to a primary care physician, the latter involves a physician-patient relationship with personalities and trust. Should the primary care physician leave one practice to go to another, there is a strong possibility that many patients will follow. That is a legitimate business interest wherein the original employer invested time and money in marketing that individual – advertising, letting people know where they are located, and perhaps paying for the physician's practice development.

Other Issues or Considerations

There are other issues to consider, too, as with a senior-tenured doctor example. In one situation, a senior doctor's leave from the employer was approved, at least initially. He had been in the practice area for more than a decade. Everyone respected him and understood he was moving on as a natural advancement in his career. Therefore, the employer told him not to worry about his relevant non-compete agreement.

However, when he was ready to depart six months later, there were less-tenured people with less-strong relationships with management and for whom the employer had a stronger legitimate business interest to enforce a non-compete (such as recent investments in them). Abruptly, the employer did an about-face with the first senior doctor and told him that it would have to enforce the non-compete against him because it would have to enforce the restrictive covenants against the junior doctors. This is one of many other issues at play or considerations by the employer when health care professionals leave.

I Know People. Should I Call Them?

"I know people, should I call them?" This is a common comment by professionals who have a good relationship with higher-up management people. The answer is, No, don't call them. They have obligations to the employer more than they do to you. And, more importantly, you need to have a plan first.

What Does It Mean to Come Up With a Plan?

We talked about this earlier in *Chapter 2*. Figure out whether you are going to negotiate or buy your way out, strategize around the restrictive covenants, such as to work in another community, or litigate your way out.

Here's a quick recap:

1. Strategize: Working within the non-compete agreement's terms to avoid its penalties.

2. Negotiate: Exchanging value with your employer to be free from the non-compete agreement.

3. Litigate: Going to court to prove your position and get out of the non-compete agreement.

This is a pivotal decision. And it's always best to make decisions when you have your rational mind. *While calm and focused, carefully analyze all the options and opportunities available to you right now.* Once word gets out about the possibility of your leaving, you will start feeling the stress. You will start feeling the pressure from peers, professional groups, and your employer. Decide early when your mind is clear and relaxed. An employment attorney can help you.

Be Careful with Friendships

Be very careful with friendships in this situation. Friendships are based on interests and a friend's professional interests may differ from yours. In speaking to someone about the possibility of leaving, you run the risk that this friend will share the information with the supervisor. (Maybe this friend is the supervisor!) Your friend's professional interests may lie more with the company, the employer, than with you.

This situation often arises when the employee believes he or she has a close friendship with the chief medical officer, CEO, or board member. "Let me call Pat the CEO. Pat's a good friend, our families get together all the time. Pat knows my situation and will understand." Stop right there. That could be risky for you.

Be mindful that the company should be treating all of its employees similarly and equally (although not necessarily identically) to avoid unlawful discrimination. It is never a great idea to bend the ear of someone with whom you have a close relationship because he or she is in a position of power, decision-making, or influence. This person also has responsibilities to the company, the employer. When an employee reaches out to a friend in this way, that individual has to balance the interests – employer vs. friend.

Using a friendship in this way may put the supervisor or CEO in a bad spot. You never want to start-off by putting someone in a bad spot. This friend may even agree with you, but that does not change the fact that he or she has an obligation, a duty, perhaps a legal obligation, to protect the company. Therefore, you should not speak with "friends" about this. Is it possible as a tactic to go speak with them? Maybe at some point, yes. But only after you have a strategy. Again, this is why you should carefully consider your options based on your unique situation.

You need a plan with action steps based on a strategy. Consulting an employment attorney can help. You will need flexibility, because rarely is the path from Step A, to B, to C a linear one. You will need to know what the pressure points are, where your leverage is, what the interests are. Then you can better analyze the situation and determine who to contact internally and when, if at all. But always come to the table prepared with a plan and a strategy.

CHAPTER 4

COST OF NEGOTIATING, LITIGATING, OR STRATEGIZING

How Can I Beat the Non-Compete? (And How Much Would It Cost?)

The number one question is "How much is it going to cost to be free of a non-compete?" Of course, no one wants to spend a lot of money on attorney's fees and legal expenses. But the truth is, we really don't know how much the cost will be because these are fact-specific situations and so much depends on the unique circumstances of your situation.

How you decide to work around or get out of the non-compete agreement – to negotiate, to litigate, or to strategize – will also have a substantial impact on the costs involved, both legal and consequential. And because there is no direct path with any of those three options, developing a legal strategy is essential. Quite simply, you need to make a plan and an employment attorney with experience with professional and executive employment law can help.

Seeking Release From the Non-Compete Agreement

Before taking any action, take time to plan and prepare a legal strategy. First, discuss with your employment attorney the probability of avoiding the non-compete agreement and the variables involved. Negotiation is the first variable that should be planned for. What are the costs in negotiating with the employer for release from the non-compete agreement?

That, too, will depend upon the health care professional's specific circumstances.

1. COST OF NEGOTIATING

An important part of any legal strategy is negotiating a settlement. How productive might those negotiations be? Does the employee have a good relationship with the employer? Are these reasonable people? Is a buyout feasible?

Does the health care professional have any other legal claims against the employer, such as a breach of contract or discrimination claim? A non-frivolous, legitimate claim against an employer may strengthen the employee's bargaining position during negotiations over terms of the non-compete agreement.

The cost of negotiations is directly tied to these questions:

- *How long would negotiations take?*

How much time will be committed to negotiations? Two weeks? Two months? Six months? A year?

- *What will negotiations look like?*

Will letters be exchanged? Will negotiations involve telephone calls? Will there be meetings? All of this takes time.

- *Will legal counsel be hired for the negotiations?*

Most times having an experienced attorney will benefit your negotiations or strategy. But, as addressing the non-compete as a business decision, conduct a cost-benefit analysis about taking on the expense of attorney representation during the negotiations with the employer.

2. COST OF LITIGATING

Choosing to litigate your way out of the non-compete agreement means having the court decide whether it is valid or enforceable. How much could litigation cost? How long would it take? By going to court, the health care professional may ask for a Declaratory Judgment declaring the non-compete to be invalid or overbroad. The employer may ask for injunctive relief in the form of a Temporary Restraining Order to stop the health care professional from working somewhere else.

Pre-Trial Temporary Restraining Order (TRO)

Another cost variable is the possibility of TRO proceedings. Although avoiding formal litigation may be preferable to both parties, this could still happen.

What if the health care professional plans to leave for another practice or health care system, but the employer does not want the professional to go to that particular employer? The employer may seek injunctive relief in the form of a temporary restraining order (TRO) to prevent the employee from working for the new employer. This is not inconsequential. TRO proceedings follow a litigant's formal request for pre-trial emergency relief to, arguably, avoid or minimize the harm caused by the employee joining the new employer until the matter is fully determined at trial. No, in New York State, an employer cannot generally force an employee to remain and work for the employer. But, yes, they may be able to prevent an employee from working for a competitive employer.

Given this is a request for emergency relief from a court, the TRO legal process moves very quickly. Attorney's fees can be high because of the time and effort required to prepare the requisite papers, the legal arguments, and the amount of time the attorney needs to devote to the client's case. As a litigant, the employer's request for a TRO against the employee is premised on the need for a court to order emergency short-term injunctive relief to prevent immediate irreparable harm caused by the health care professional's resignation, including the costs to provide patient care in the employee's absence or the loss of profits caused by the employee departing.

Here are a few rules of thumb with any TRO or litigation. Any emergency relief or TRO battle could easily cost $15,000, $25,000, or more. Many non-compete litigations end with a settlement at the TRO phase. But several do not end there and the cost of litigating a full case over a year or more, no matter how simple or complex the possible lawsuit's issues may be, could be at least $120,000 *prior to a trial*. Of course, you don't want to spend that much money *unless* you realize it is the cost of doing business. As we've discussed, this has to be a rational decision. Is leaving the employer and litigating the non-compete agreement a solid business decision? If you are going to profit by doing so, then maybe litigation costs are worth it.

3. COST OF STRATEGIZING

The third option is to strategize a way to leave the employer and work around the non-compete agreement. This involves analyzing the employer's rights and building an optimal compliance plan around those rights, mostly as to time and distance restrictions.

The costs associated with strategizing your way around it tend to be more personal time, but commuting costs factor in, too. Is there a practice outside of the restricted geographical limits where you could work? How much time and money would be involved in commuting there each week? What would the personal cost be to you for traveling farther than you do now?

If you can consider all of the involved factors and sustain those costs for the length of the non-compete terms, then it may be a good option for you.

How Much Am I Willing to Spend to Get Out of the Non-Compete?

No matter which of the three options or what combination of the three you consider, there will be costs involved. Let's be honest, no one wants to spend a lot of money on attorneys. Believe me, I understand that point. The reality is, however, that nobody knows what the true cost of litigating the non-compete agreement will be. There are no promises, no guarantees. Therefore, it is a good idea to assess all options and create a plan that works best for you, based on your timeline, your financial situation, and how you handle the stress of the situation. Then you can confidently move forward in your career. Make this key financial decision before the stress of your employment situation sets in.

How Do the Numbers Add Up?

Put personal relationships within the hospital or medical practice aside and view this decision as the cost of doing business. How do the scales balance? On one side is the cost of getting out of the non-compete agreement. On the other side is the ability to profit more and/or to achieve your professional career goals and financial positions you desire for your family.

There is a cost to negotiating or litigating or strategizing your way around the non-compete agreement. Talk to an employment law attorney with experience litigating non-competes and other restrictive covenants. Learn and set your limits and financial boundaries (remember, you don't need all of the funds up front) and analyze the range of costs associated with each option. It could be cheaper to strategize around the non-compete and work in a neighboring city, or to buy your way out by paying the employer, but it might make business sense to litigate to ensure that you can earn a greater compensation from a new employer.

CHAPTER 5

OTHER RESTRICTIVE COVENANTS

What Are the Other Restrictive Covenants and Why Are They Important?

In this chapter, we shift the conversation to other restrictive covenants in employment agreements – the covenant not to solicit patients and covenant not to solicit employees. These are very popular restrictive covenants that are more typically enforced than non-compete agreements. Both can further complicate the health care professional's decision to leave the current employer.

Non-Solicitation of Patients

A restrictive covenant to not solicit patients in an employment agreement typically states, in effect, that for a reasonable amount of time, the employee promises not to "directly" or "indirectly" solicit patients to follow that health care professional to the new employer or new practice.

What Does It Mean to Not Solicit Patients?

The non-solicitation of patients generally comes down to two restrictions:

Examples of direct solicitation prohibitions:

1. Do not market to specific patients, or

2. Do not invite or otherwise encourage patients to visit you at the new employer or new practice.

Examples of indirect solicitation prohibitions:

1. Do not ask your professional colleague to encourage patients to contact your new office, or

2. Do not provide a list of patient names and contact information to your new practice, which then sends letters directly to the patient inviting them to contact you at the new practice.

Once again, this is a fact specific analysis and will depend on your unique circumstances.

Which Acts Are Permissible?

Broad *general mass marketing* in various publications, such as trade journals and newspapers, even social media, is permissible because mass marketing is not targeted at any specific patient. The line is crossed into patient solicitation, and perhaps prohibited territory, the moment the health care professional implements *direct marketing* by sending letters, emailing, or using social media to reach patients directly.

What if a prior patient happens to see the mass general advertisement and happens to contact the new practice? Generally speaking, in that instance the prior patient may be accepted by the new practice as a patient and be treated without the restrictive covenant being violated.

What If My Patient Reaches Out to Me?

Sometimes a patient will initiate communication about following the health care professional to his or her new employer. When the patient calls to say, "Doctor, I'd like to follow you to your new practice, where are you going?" it isn't considered a direct solicitation by you because the patient reached out to you; the patient initiated the contact. Be mindful, however, under certain circumstances such an interaction could become an indirect solicitation of a patient and may possibly violate the non-solicitation covenant. Sometimes the better course of action is to respond with something along the lines of, "I appreciate your interest. However, I'm contractually prohibited from soliciting you. But if you're interested in changing practices, you are free to contact the main office of my new practice at this number." And say no more.

What About Keeping Patients Informed?

As you know, in New York State doctors and dentists have an ethical obligation to keep those patients who are under a course of treatment apprised of the doctor's or dentist's whereabouts. How will this duty to keep patients informed be satisfied? Typically, the current employer promises to send a letter to the patients.

The letter indicates that, although the patient's doctor or dentist is changing practices, the current employer will continue to care for the patient and will assign that patient a new doctor or dentist. Near the end of the letter is usually a sentence stating, "If you wish to change practices, when we are presented with the proper authorization signed by you, we will transfer your records," or similar language.

Employers prefer to send these letters to patients because they can control the messaging. The employer wants to control when and how patients are notified of the professional's departure and does not want to have the professional solicit the patient for the new practice. Of course, the professional may wish to send the notice of practice transfer, but that professional should be mindful of how he or she obtains the patient contact information because it very likely may be deemed confidential information by the employer. Therefore, it is always wise to seek legal advice prior to accessing employer records for patient contact information.

How Long Will This Go On?

In their final month or week of employment, many health care professionals love to tell their patients, "By the way, I'm leaving and this is where I'm going." Resist the temptation. Telling a patient where you're moving to next could violate a non-solicitation agreement.

A reasonable non-solicitation of patients period typically lasts 12 to 24 months. Yes, it can be challenging to not say a word to your patients about leaving the current practice. But saying nothing about it until after you've parted ways is typically the safest, most legally defensible, position to take.

When the employer takes on the responsibility of sending the practice change notice to patients informing them of the health care professional's departure from the practice, it may be possible for the doctor or dentist to review it and make comments to the employer before it's finalized and mailed. A good employer should allow this review, although they don't necessarily have to.

On the other side of this will be the new employer's marketing initiatives to welcome the health care professional to the new practice. Be ready to answer a patient's inquiry about where you're moving to with something along the lines of, "I'm contractually prohibited from soliciting you, but I'm sure that my whereabouts will be publicized soon on social media or in the newspaper," or something to that effect. This puts the onus on the patient to keep an eye out for mass marketing from the new employer.

Non-Solicitation Of Employees

What Is Non-Solicitation Of Employees?

Simply put, if you are leaving Practice-A to go to Practice-B, then you are agreeing not to solicit other employees at Practice-A to join you at Practice-B. It matters not whether the other employee is a doctor, physician assistant, nurse, nurse practitioner, other health care professional, or staff. Because they are all employees of Practice-A, you cannot solicit any of them. A reasonable period of non-solicitation of employees is also 12 to 24 months, typically.

What If Former Co-Workers Respond to My New Employer's Job Vacancy Announcements?

People are free to respond to job postings, of course. However, be very careful about what is said to a former co-worker who calls you because he or she has an interview with your new employer and just wants to ask a few questions about, "What's it like there?" Understand that sharing your experiences with the new employer and explaining the culture of the new employer is fine. But remember not to say, "You should come" or "You would enjoy it here" or make any statement that could be misconstrued as soliciting the former co-worker, directly or indirectly. (Directly or indirectly are similar in the employee solicitation provision as they are in the patient solicitation provision.)

MEDICAL PRACTICE OWNERS

What If I Own an Interest in the Practice and Want to Leave?

If the health care professional has an ownership interest in a professional limited liability partnership (PLLP) or professional limited liability company (PLLC) or is a shareholder in a professional corporation (PC), or other business entity, then more than one ownership agreement or governing document may include a non-compete or another restrictive covenant.

What If I Am a Practice Partner?

A partner should not be accepting patients or business in direct competition with the current entity. Each partner owes fiduciary duties, or responsibilities, to the other partners (or other shareholders) in certain circumstances. Each partner has an obligation not to usurp corporate opportunities. The health care professional who is an owner or practice partner and an employee (even in the absence of an employment agreement) should not be competing against the current entity. Under limited circumstances this may be possible, but it is a very rare occurrence.

Non-Compete in the Employment Agreement

Even though the health care professional may be a practice owner, he or she will likely have a non-compete in an employment agreement with the business entity. An employment agreement for the entity functions the same way as for any other employee. Yes, you may own the entity or have an equity ownership in the entity, but the entity itself is considered to be a party with rights.

Other restrictive covenants in an employment agreement are also likely, such as the non-solicitation of patients and non-solicitation of employees. Depending on the entity form – PLLC, PLLP, PC, or any other – restrictive covenants may be in the organizational documents (i.e. the shareholders' agreement, members' agreement, operating agreement) or in some other agreement that includes owner responsibilities and obligations to the independent entity and to any co-owners.

Non-Compete in the Buy-Sell Agreement

Typically, a practice partner will have a Buy-Sell Agreement in the entity's governing documents. This means that if the partner is leaving, then he or she must sell the entity interest back to the entity. This agreement may also contain a restrictive covenant. Similarly, there would likely be restrictive covenant obligations when selling an interest in the practice to a third party, such as a new health care professional joining the practice, too.

The Little Known Mohawk Doctrine

Health care professionals also need to be aware of a particular legal theory in New York State called the *Mohawk Doctrine*. The Mohawk Doctrine is a common law rule that places on the seller of a business in New York a non-solicitation of patients (or customers) restrictive covenant, which means the seller of the business interest is bound by a non-solicitation of patients restrictive covenant with or without a written agreement. Why, you wonder? Because, simply stated, it is a means to protect the "goodwill" of the business or practice that is being sold to another party. Even if a non-solicitation of patients term is not written in the sale documents, a court will likely find that the Mohawk Doctrine applies and you are restricted from soliciting those patients. For how long, you wonder?

Indefinitely.

In the next chapter, we will talk about planning your transition to the new employer or new practice.

CHAPTER 6

NEW PRACTICE, NEW CONSIDERATIONS

What Should I Do When Leaving One Practice for the Next?

Now that you have decided to change positions, there is much for which you need to prepare. Changing employers is an important career move for any health care professional. Give the discussion points presented in this chapter due consideration and talk to your attorney for clarification and assistance.

When changing employers, ensure that you:

1. Have a plan.

2. Be prepared to answer your current employer's questions and make your departure plan presentation as innocuous as possible.

3. Do not solicit patients while still employed because of the risk of violating your non-solicitation agreement or the *Faithless Servant Doctrine*.

4. Do not talk about leaving to colleagues or try to solicit other employees to join you.

Let's start by planning to give notice that you are leaving the current practice.

1. HAVE A PLAN

You will give notice to your employer before informing your patients that you are leaving the current practice. There is a right way and wrong way to carry out both of those tasks.

Whether an attorney is consulted (this is strongly encouraged) or not, you will need a well-considered plan for what you are going to do, how and when you are going to do it, what you are going to say to your supervisor, and what you are not going to say to others. When you break the news, you need to be prepared to answer your employer's questions, many of which can be anticipated – so be prepared.

When and How Do I Give Notice to My Employer?

Plan when and how to give notice to your employer of your move to the new practice. There are two important aspects to this timing issue:

- **What does the employment agreement say?**

The health care professional should plan to satisfy any contractual obligations and give sufficient notice to satisfy any contractual obligation regarding the same, whether it's 90 days or six-months notice. (Reasonable notice is discussed in *Chapter 2*.)

- **What is the relocation plan?**

The health care professional should not give notice to the employer until there is a firm plan to execute. Don't put the cart before the horse!

In general, the best answer to the question – "When should I give notice?" – is to provide the minimum notice required by the employment contract or as deemed professionally appropriate for the treatment of the patients.

Take the high road, especially if you're in the early or midpoint of your professional career. Be professional and simply say face-to-face (or you could submit an email), "I've really enjoyed my time here and I've learned a lot. However, please accept this as my notice that I'll be leaving the practice. I will of course work with the practice to determine the best date for my last day, but I anticipate my last day to be," and provide a date.

Does it matter whether the health care professional had a great experience with this employer or a poor one? No, not really. Having said that, there is the professional community of which to be mindful. Professional circles tend to be very small, even when the community in which the person lives or practices is a large one. There may be talk about you changing employment, but it probably won't be to the extent you may think. Colleagues are likely to do some commenting because they have a professional interest in who's leaving and why.

When and How Do I Inform Patients of My Move to the New Practice?

By now, it should be fairly obvious that a mere mention of your move prematurely, even an unintentional slip-up, could become problematic. So when and how should the health care professional start informing patients about the move to a new practice?

The safest answer is to wait until you are no longer employed by your current employer before mentioning your move. Thereafter, depending on the nuances of your specific situation, you or your new employer may start advertising that you changed practices with an announcement or messaging similar to – "I've joined this new practice and I'm now accepting new patients." Only when permitted to solicit patients (depending on the termination of the restrictive covenant or settlement of that issue) should the health care professional send letters or other notices directly to patients or contact them on social media.

Limitations on Advertising and Marketing

Let's assume the health care professional has a non-compete, but the new practice is outside of the geographical limitations. Or maybe the non-compete is not in effect, but there is a non-solicit provision. In those situations, using *general mass advertising* is always the safest path, whether it's the local business paper, local medical journal, association newsletter, or social media. It's always wiser to advertise generally and not to reach out directly to patients. Even with social media marketing, it's never a good idea to target prior patients specifically or to encourage prior patients to come to the new practice.

Remember, too, the doctor's ethical obligation in New York to keep patients informed of the doctor's whereabouts. As a doctor, you have the right and ability to send out notices directly to all patients under your treatment to inform them of your relocation. This is true for dentists, as well. But, as mentioned above, be considerate of the methods and messaging used. Remember, as discussed in *Chapter 5*, many employers prefer to send these letters to patients on your behalf in order to control the messaging.

Patient Records and Medical Progress Notes
Can I Bring My Patient Records With Me?

Although the patient record belongs to the patient (arguably, at least a copy of it does), the general rule in New York is for health care professionals to not bring patient records to the new practice. This has more to do with medical record technology than with anything else.

The law is clear in that health care providers can bring their patient records to the new practice. But which records belong to the health care provider and which belong to the practice? Digital patient record management and storage has made this less clear from a practical standpoint. Patient records are typically stored in digital form on the employer's computer system and, therefore, belong to the employer. Hence, the general rule is not to bring your patient records to the new practice.

Records Transfer Procedure

Before patients begin contacting the health care professional at the new practice, procedures should be in place to transfer patient records from the previous practice to the new practice. If the patient chooses to follow the doctor to the new practice, then the patient is typically required to sign a consent or release form permitting the current practice to send the records to the new practice. The previous employer may require the patient to come into the office to sign for and pick-up the records personally, and also take responsibility for delivering them to the new practice. It may not be good customer service, but it is a practice used.

2. BE PREPARED TO ANSWER THE EMPLOYER'S QUESTIONS AND MAKE YOUR PRESENTATION AS INNOCUOUS AS POSSIBLE

You may expect your employer to either be genuinely saddened or genuinely happy for you by the news of your departure, but that's not always the case. Think about this from the employer's perspective. The supervisor's first concern is, "How are we going to service these patients?" The second concern is, "Will we be able to keep these patients?" A third concern may be, "Who else is going to leave now?" The employer will be thinking about the business entity and how it benefits from the employment relationship with the physician, nurse, dentist, or other health care professional who is leaving.

The employer is going to take whatever lawful action is necessary to protect its interests and may make statements to the effect of, "Don't say anything to the patients and we'll get back to you." The supervisor may pose questions right away, "Where are you going?" and "What will you be doing?" and the health care professional should be prepared with appropriate, honest answers that do not violate the employment agreement. Do not be caught unprepared. Take the time to rehearse this scene in your mind. It's easy to fall into the trap of sharing information that could negatively affect you as you're trying to depart. They call it an "exit strategy" for a reason. Have a plan for what information you will share and won't share, and anticipate as many questions as possible.

3. DO NOT SOLICIT PATIENTS WHILE STILL EMPLOYED (OR FACE THE RISK OF VIOLATING THE FAITHLESS SERVANT DOCTRINE)

What Is New York's Faithless Servant Doctrine?

The employed New York health care professional should be careful about speaking directly to patients about the planned departure prior to leaving the employer. While most employment agreements state that you cannot compete or solicit while employed by the employer, there is also a common law prohibition against such acts in New York State known as the *Faithless Servant Doctrine.*

In essence, the Faithless Servant Doctrine says the employee cannot compete with his or her employer *while still employed* there. Under this common law (meaning that there is no contractual obligation, but a legal prohibition nonetheless), the health care professional cannot work by day at the employer's practice and operate a competing practice by night (or weekend) with the employee profiting alone. "Moonlighting," as it's often called, can get people into trouble under the common law.

Typically, an anti-moonlighting provision is included in an employment agreement. But even in the absence of an employment agreement, the employee who competes against the employer during his or her time of employment will violate New York's Faithless Servant Doctrine. Why? A simple explanation is that an employee is supposed to devote fulltime efforts to support the employer's business without the employer being concerned that the employee would redirect a customer, here a patient, to a competing practice and deny the employer the profit. Similarly, an employee who is about to leave the employer for a competing practice cannot siphon away the employer's patients. Those are the legalities of the situation; the realities of it may surprise you.

Violating the Faithless Servant Doctrine is not inconsequential. There are damages for doing so. The employer could be entitled to disgorgement of the doctor's compensation for the entire period that the doctor was violating the Faithless Servant Doctrine. Thus, you should be mindful of this risk and not advertise your move.

4. DO NOT TALK TO COLLEAGUES ABOUT LEAVING

It's natural to experience a sense of relief after submitting your resignation. The stress lifts, the future looks bright. You may feel happy and relaxed for the first time in a long while, but be circumspect. Be mindful of what news you share, with whom you share it, and how it is presented. For example, saying something to the effect of, "I'm leaving for this wonderful other practice with greater opportunities," could be considered disparaging by the employer, or an attempt to have other employees ask you about the new practice in order to improperly solicit them. Certainly don't say anything like, "You should come apply, too," because that is a more explicit solicitation.

Even if you do not have a non-solicitation covenant, nothing puts you on the employer's radar faster than "corporate raiding," as some managers or owners consider it to be. If such discussions occur or more people start leaving at the same time you do, then the employer may become stricter in how they manage your exit. The better course is to be professional and respectful in the situation and try to avoid becoming the center of attention.

CHAPTER 7

DISCRIMINATION IN A NUTSHELL

What About Discrimination in the Workplace?

So far, everything we've discussed has assumed there is reasonably respectful treatment in the work environment where the health care professional is employed. Unfortunately, that is not always the case. On occasion, a health care professional's move may be prompted by actual unlawful discrimination against that professional. Or there might be retaliation against that professional for coming forward with a complaint about some instance of perceived or actual unlawful discrimination.

The laws involved with these two related topics – workplace discrimination and retaliation – can be complex and recently have been evolving frequently in New York State. To go into substantive detail is beyond the scope of this book. There is another Glennon Guide on this topic that addresses more closely these workplace concerns, the various state and federal employment laws meant to address these problems, and the judicial interpretations of those state and federal laws. For our purposes here – that is, from the perspective of the non-compete agreement in the health care field – we'll summarize these issues generally for you.

Please remember that the discrimination and retaliation inquiry will always require a fact specific analysis that is unique to you. Just as the restrictive covenants that apply to your employment are unique to you.

Is All Discrimination or Retaliation at the Workplace Unlawful?

No. There are lawful employer acts and there are unlawful employer acts. Let's begin with what is lawful.

Although it is unpleasant or hurtful to be on the receiving end, as well as being unwanted and inappropriate, the reality is that harassing, bullying, treating employees poorly, and exercising poor management skills are generally legal. The only time such improper behavior becomes illegal or unlawful is when that harassment, bullying, or poor treatment is being done because of a trait that falls under a legally protected category.

What Are Protected Categories?

There are federal laws that created age, gender, race, color, religion, national origin, and disability, among other protected categories. There are also New York State laws that created those same protected categories, as well as more, including sexual orientation and military status, among others.

In certain circumstances, under both legal frameworks, there are also protections based on familial relationships and dress preferences, if they are related to culture or religion, among other things.

While both federal and New York State laws are generally (but not always) interpreted the same way, New York State changed its legal standard for determining unlawful discrimination and harassment (effective October 29, 2020). Now the New York employee or job applicant has an easier standard to prove discrimination, at least easier than the federal standard which requires "severe or pervasive" discrimination. New York dropped the higher "severe or pervasive" standard and now requires only that the alleged harassment or retaliation rise above the level of "petty slights and trivial inconveniences." This effectively removes the burden of proving "severe or pervasive" comments, acts, or omissions against the employee, under New York law. In its essence, an example of the difference between New York law and federal law may be generalized as an employer's single comment, one single remark, may not constitute harassment under the more difficult standard of proof in the federal law. But under New York's recent change in the law, a single comment may possibly be sufficient to state a claim due to the lower standard. Notably, there are other changes to New York State's discrimination laws that favor the employee, but they are not addressed in this Glennon Guide.

Has the Employer's Behavior Risen to the Level of Actionable Discrimination?

Being teased by the employer about wearing an "ugly sweater" or being harassed because of the social activities you engaged in or your favorite sports team is not generally unlawful. Annoying and obnoxious, perhaps. But unlawful? Not usually.

There is no law prohibiting an employer or supervisor from simply being unprofessional or a jerk. I'm fond of saying, "If you're a New England Patriots fan, not only could you be fired, but you should be fired" and that comment is legal. Similarly, a supervisor constantly commenting about your slow work production or your incessant chattiness throughout the workday is also lawful. On their own, these comments are permissible.

However, when the employer constantly comments about your gender, dating life, sex life, or how age is slowing you down and it's "impossible to teach an old dog new tricks," or makes comments about religious headwear, any of those comments could be unlawful harassment rising to the level of an unlawful, hostile work environment. Arguably, such harassment could be the basis for a claim of *constructive discharge*. This is important, because constructive discharge could invalidate an otherwise valid non-compete or other restrictive covenant because constructive discharge may be viewed by a court as the same as the employer terminating the employee. (See *Chapter 3* for a discussion on constructive discharge.)

How Is Unlawful Retaliation Tied to Employment Discrimination?

If you complained about alleged unlawful discrimination and that complaint resulted in an adverse employment action – meaning you lost compensation, received less scheduled work or fewer shifts, had responsibilities reduced or stature diminished – then you may have been unlawfully retaliated against.

Retaliation occurs when a negative action is taken by the employer against the health care professional after that employee complained of unlawful discrimination, harassment, or a hostile work environment based on a lawfully protected category. Retaliation can be actionable even if the unlawful discrimination complained of did not rise to the level of being unlawful. The fact that an employee in a protected category complained about discrimination to the employer and, thereafter, the employee received an adverse employment action or negative treatment from the employer; that may be sufficient for a claim of retaliation.

Consider an example of a complaint followed by negative action: In April, the health care professional complained to the employer, "I'm being picked on for my gender" (gender being a protected category), but the alleged ill treatment didn't rise to the level of unlawful harassment. In May, the employee gets demoted and his or her compensation is reduced. The fact that the employee complained about being harassed based on a protected category and later suffered the adverse employment action of demotion and reduced compensation could be considered unlawful retaliation if they are directly related. Of course, if the demotion and pay reduction were actually due to poor performance, as the employer would claim, then there would be no retaliation. The specific facts matter to the analysis.

Is there a retaliation claim for the health care professional who complained about being teased for liking a certain sports team (not a protected category) and who then suffers an adverse employment action? No, that would be lawful retaliation. It may be the employer's idea of payback, but it's likely lawful retaliation. Remember, there's no law against the company you work for being unprofessional.

How Else Could Discrimination Law Apply to Non-Competes?

How the employer chooses to enforce the non-compete against the health care professional may form the basis for unlawful discrimination or unlawful retaliation based on that employer's actions in the unique facts and circumstances of the situation.

Does the employer enforce these non-competes only against one gender? Are non-competes only enforced against the younger doctors who are just beginning to build their practices; or only against the older doctors with stronger practices? These are examples of the kinds of facts that could form the basis, or foundation, for discrimination in the application or enforcement of the health care professional's restricted covenants.

Do I Need an Attorney?

Analyzing whether unlawful discrimination or an unlawful hostile work environment exists, on the one hand, and whether such unlawful discrimination constitutes *constructive discharge*, on the other hand, are both fact-based determinations requiring analysis by an attorney. Does any of this resonate with you and your employment experience? Do you feel that you are being subjected to unlawful discrimination or retaliation? We strongly encourage you to seek guidance by contacting an experienced employment attorney with whom you can discuss the details.

CHAPTER 8

CONCLUSION: SUGGESTIONS TO AVOID NON-COMPETE ISSUES

When Should I Contact an Attorney?

Contact an attorney prior to signing an agreement containing a non-compete or other restrictive covenant; or before you decide or announce to change employers. We all know the adage "an ounce of prevention" and its meaning. Prevention is what we are encouraging as the best way to manage the risks associated with non-compete agreements and other restrictive covenants. Otherwise, you may find yourself in a high-pressure situation and need to hire an attorney to assist in negotiating, settling, or litigating.

You should also consider each of the points raised in the previous chapters.

In *Chapter 1*, we started the discussion about non-compete agreements by describing three scenarios in which you and most health care professionals will find themselves. Those are:

First Scenario:
You are getting ready to sign your first (or a new) employment agreement with a restrictive covenant or non-compete.

Second Scenario:
You are contemplating leaving your position and want to better understand your current employment agreement.

Third Scenario:
>You plan to leave your position, but have reason to believe your current employer will object to the new employer of your choice. Or you already resigned your position and are experiencing unanticipated challenges in obtaining employment because of the non-compete or other restrictive covenant.

What differs in the legal analysis for each scenario? Timing. That is, timing to devise and implement a personal strategy to best approach resolving the issues. The best approach is to carefully think about career issues ahead of time, prior to signing the employment agreement. You should obtain advice from counsel before making any key decision and certainly before announcing your departure from the medical practice.

At The Glennon Law Firm, P.C., we discuss various strategies with our clients. By learning about the legal options available to them, our clients are able to take greater control of their professional careers. Personal strategies win every time. With proper planning of your personal strategy, you can avoid paying, being beholden to, or litigating a non-compete with a current or past employer.

What If I'm Negotiating an Agreement Now?

There are two career moments when you should take time to assess what is happening and what may happen – before signing an employment agreement and before resigning your position with the employer. In both of those situations, you are in full control and not simply reacting to other pressures.

Are you in the process of negotiating an employment agreement? It's never too early to start thinking about how the terms of a non-compete agreement may affect your future. Before signing one is the best time. This moment in your career is your opportunity to control the possible future negative effects of a non-compete. Have an experienced attorney review the proposed contract and spot any issues.

An experienced attorney should ask you what your professional and personal goals are for the timeframe that you will be employed there and for the term of any restrictive covenant thereafter. If you start to plan early, before deciding whether to accept the position, then you may be able to adjust the agreement more to your benefit.

What If I Already Have an Agreement?

If you do not pay close attention to the possible impact on future career alternatives before signing the non-compete agreement, if you simply sign on the dotted line, then your attorney will have to work to attempt to get you out of it. Initially, this may involve negotiating the terms of the non-compete, such as the geographic limit, duration, or types of employment in which you are free to engage. This may involve buying your way out of the non-compete by settling with the employer for a financial sum in order for you to be free to move on. Getting out of the non-compete may involve litigation, fighting the non-compete in court by challenging its enforceability against you. Lastly, leaving the current practice may involve strategizing a way out by accepting a new position that allows the non-compete time period to expire so you do not violate it – in other words, live with it.

At the very minimum, always obtain legal advice before raising the topic of changing employment with your current employer. Before taking action on your own, learn what will trigger the non-compete provision in the agreement.

When you already have an employment agreement and are contemplating the pros and cons of making a job change, plan early before deciding to make that change. Always consider your options and have a plan *before* giving notice to your employer. You don't want to implement an important career change before you have a plan.

Yes, sometimes great professional opportunities pop-up at the last minute. In that instance, I would strongly encourage you to contact an attorney before taking action. The better course is to think this through, to have a plan, and to keep the matter confidential. I know everybody trusts somebody else, but guess what? Somebody else trusts somebody else, and so on it goes. As you contemplate the benefits and detriments of making a job change, keep your plans confidential.

Contact an attorney who can help provide you with a roadmap. Because you are currently working under an employment contract, you need someone to analyze the specific issues involved in your leaving the current employer and assist you in devising a plan before you actually resign. You need someone to analyze the issues before you submit your resignation. Someone who can help you map out your exit, advise and help you articulate your plans and, if need be, guide you through this career transition.

At The Glennon Law Firm, P.C., the first step we take is to assess your goals and analyze your options, create a personal strategy for you, then make suggestions based on what we believe is the best path forward. Then you make a decision.

What happens next? The statement I made at the beginning of this book is worth repeating here: "When we see the path, you need only take my hand, put your head down, and follow me. We will get you through the forest. Yes, it can be a bumpy ride. But by planning appropriately, we can anticipate those bumps and get you over them, one by one."

THE GLENNON LAW FIRM, P.C.
160 LINDEN OAKS
ROCHESTER, NY 14625

585-210-2150

GLENNONLAWFIRM.COM

Made in the USA
Middletown, DE
04 March 2023